I0478463

School Teachers Swear Adult Coloring Book

This Coloring book belongs to:

____

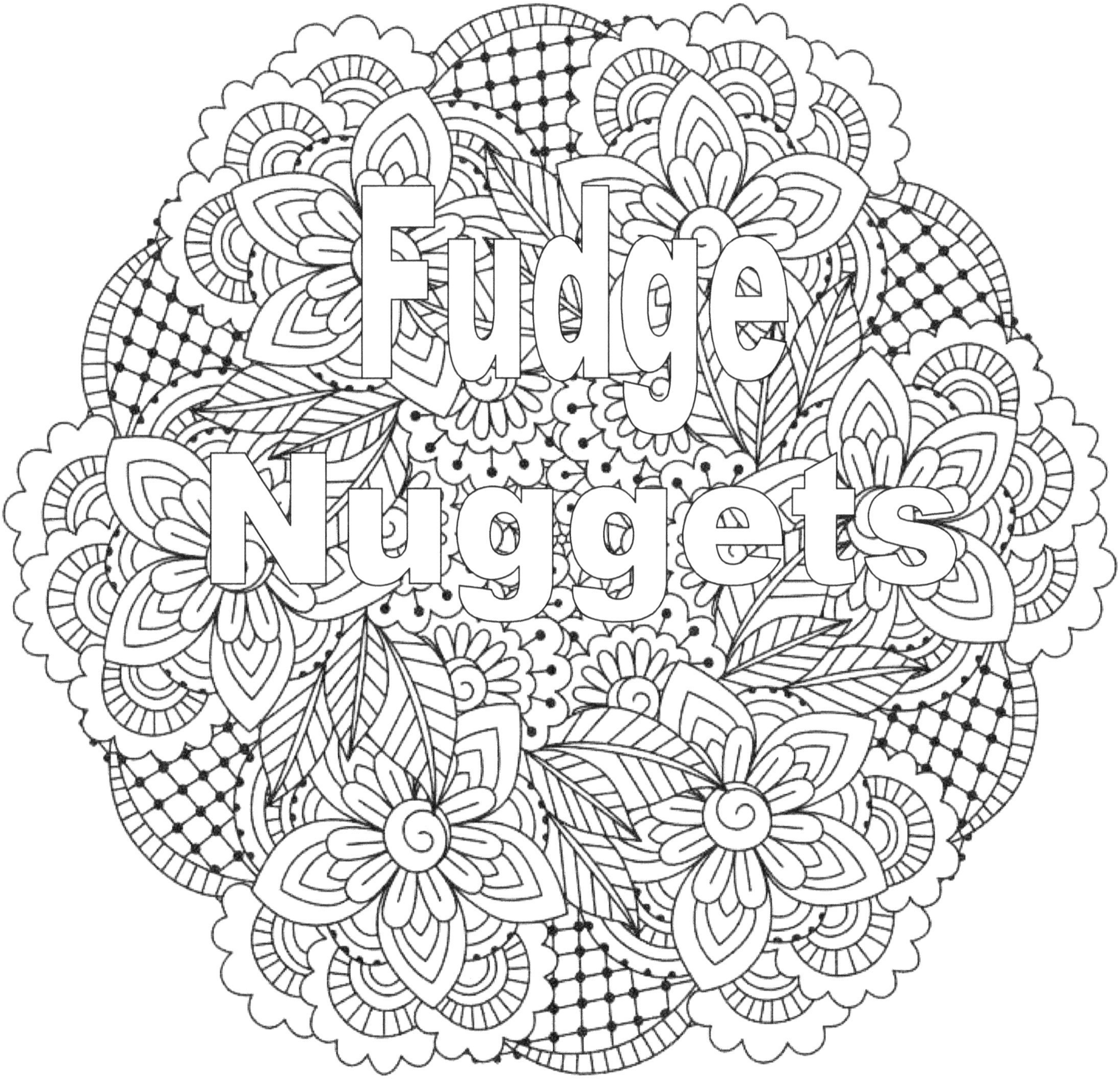
Fudge
Nuggets

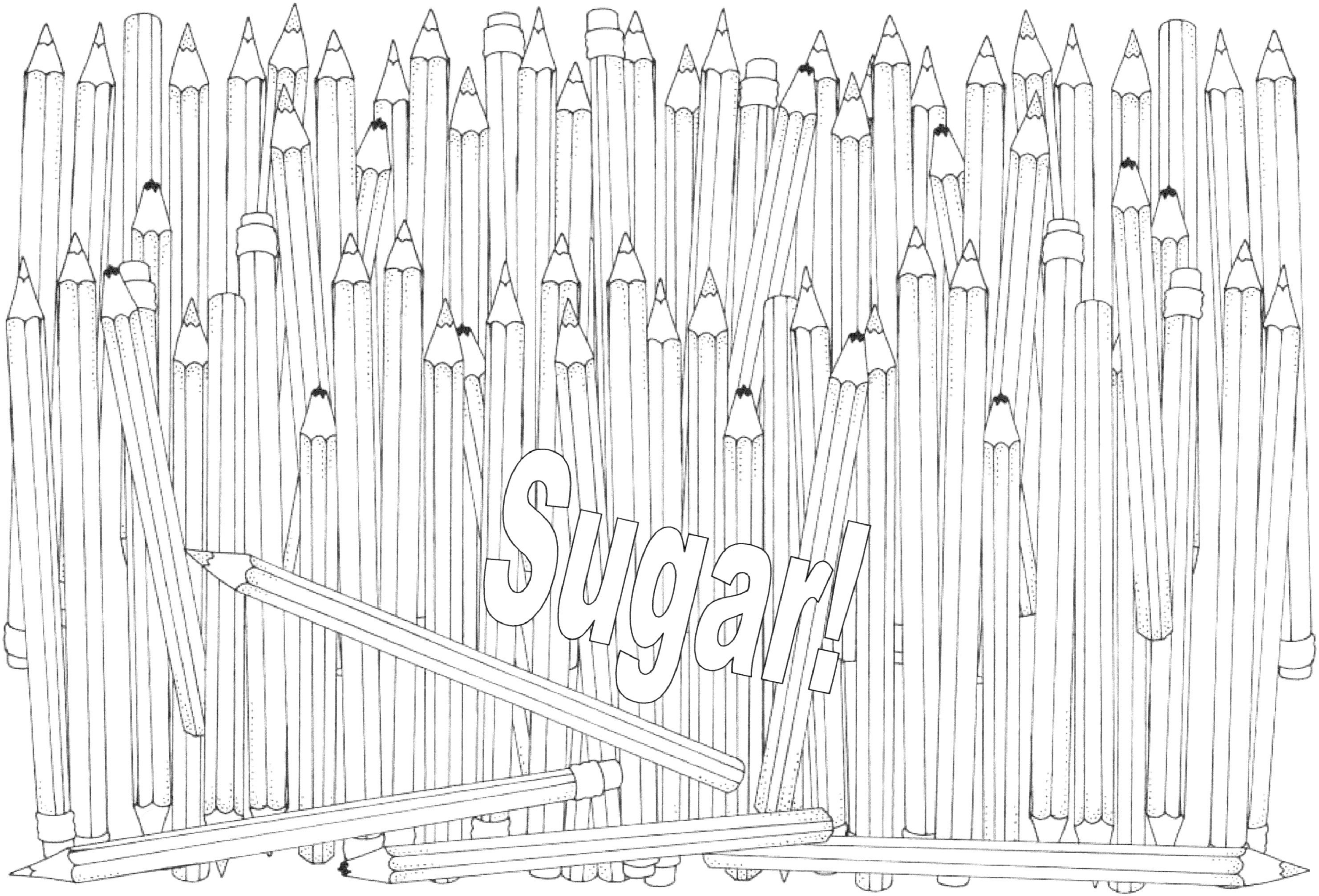
Sugar!

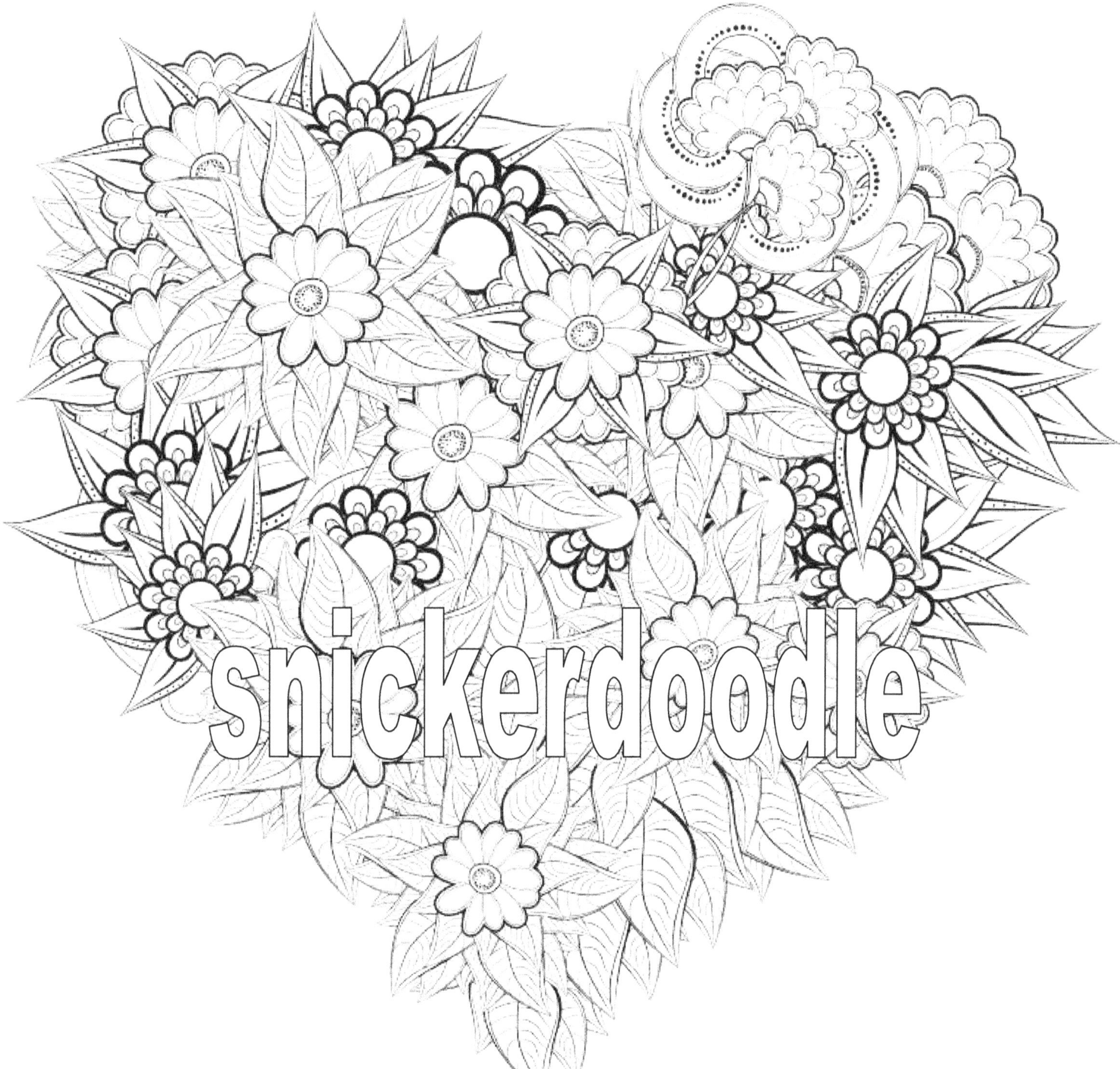
snickerdoodle

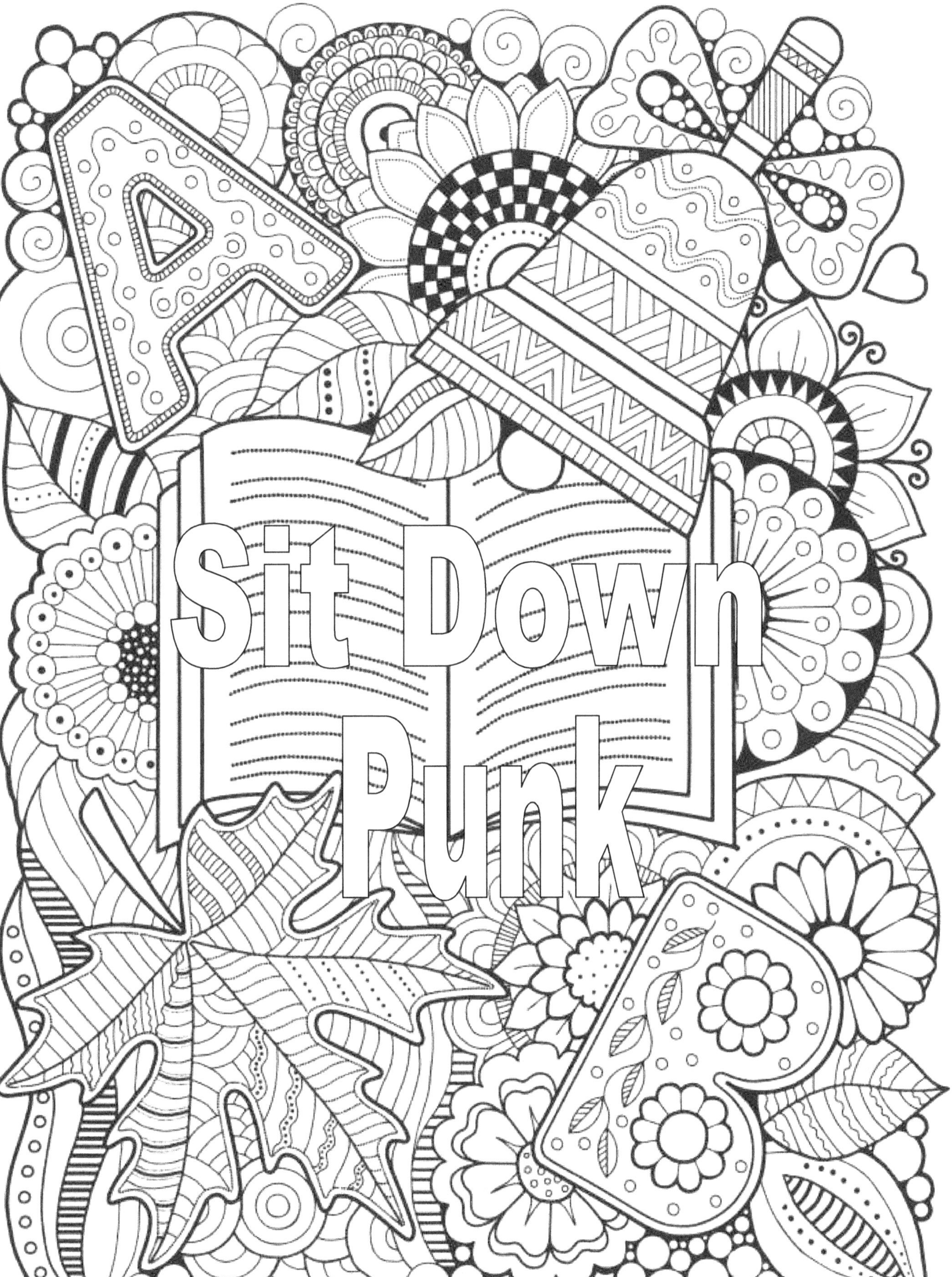
Sit Down
Punk

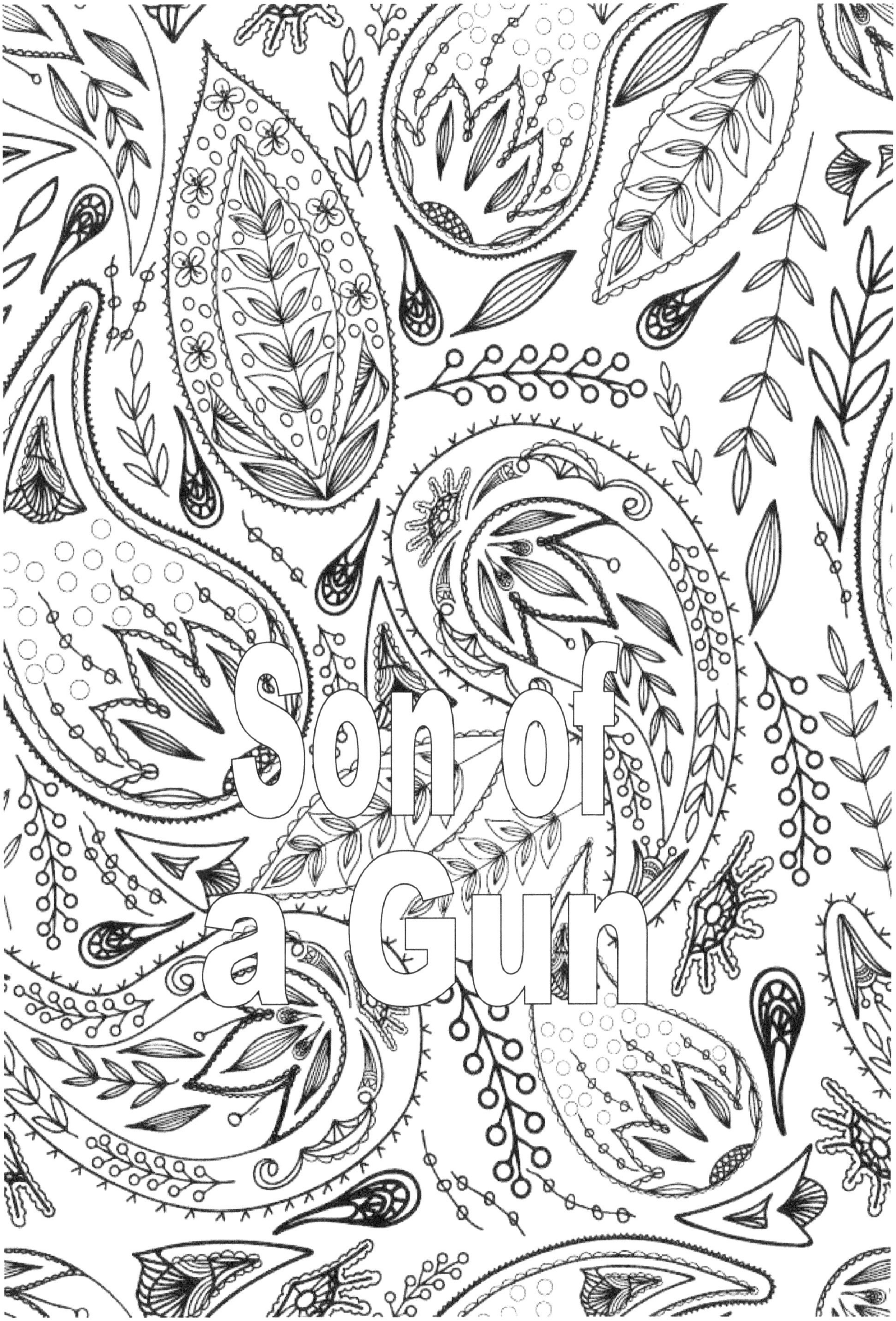
Son of
a Gun

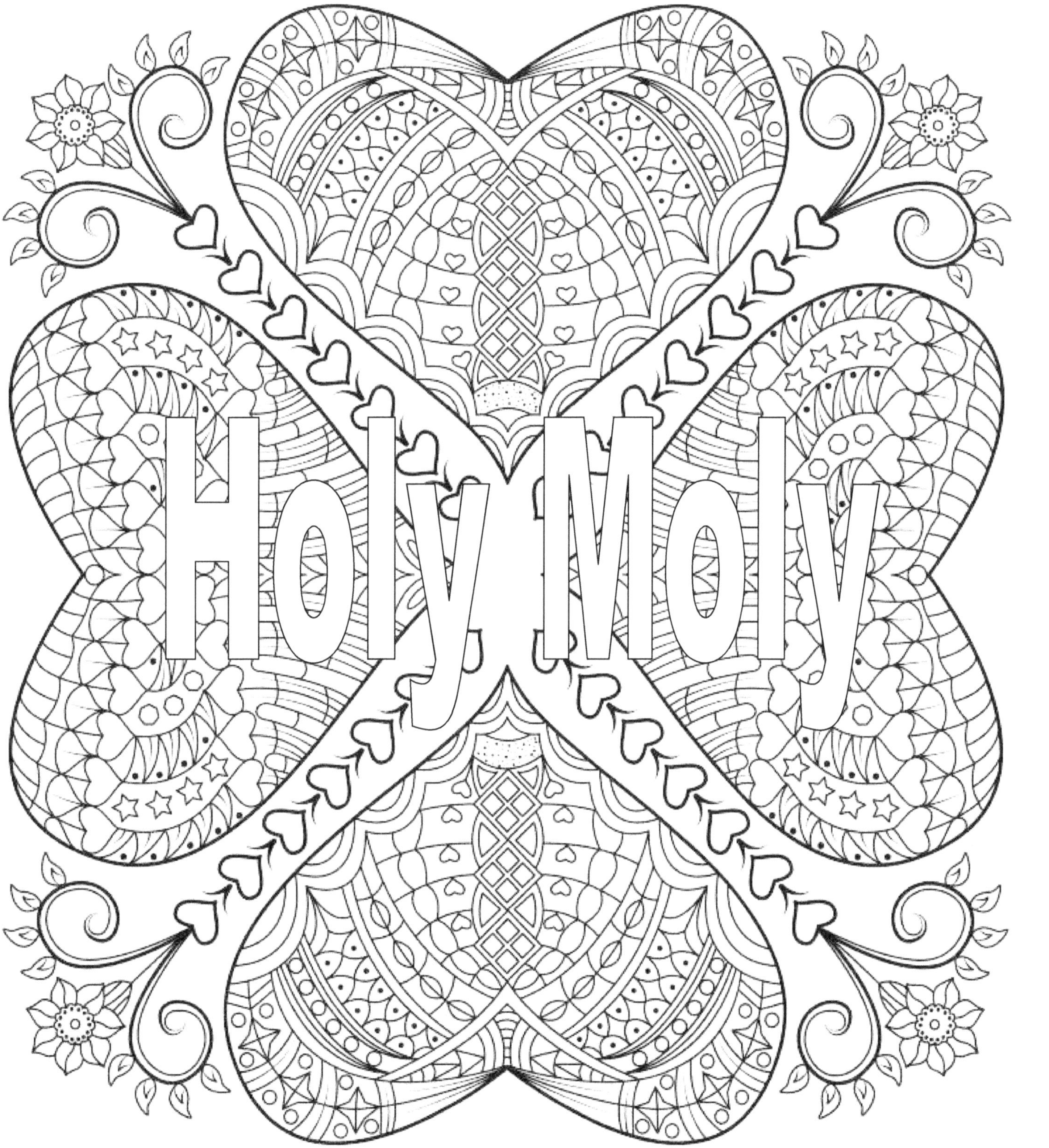
Holy Moly

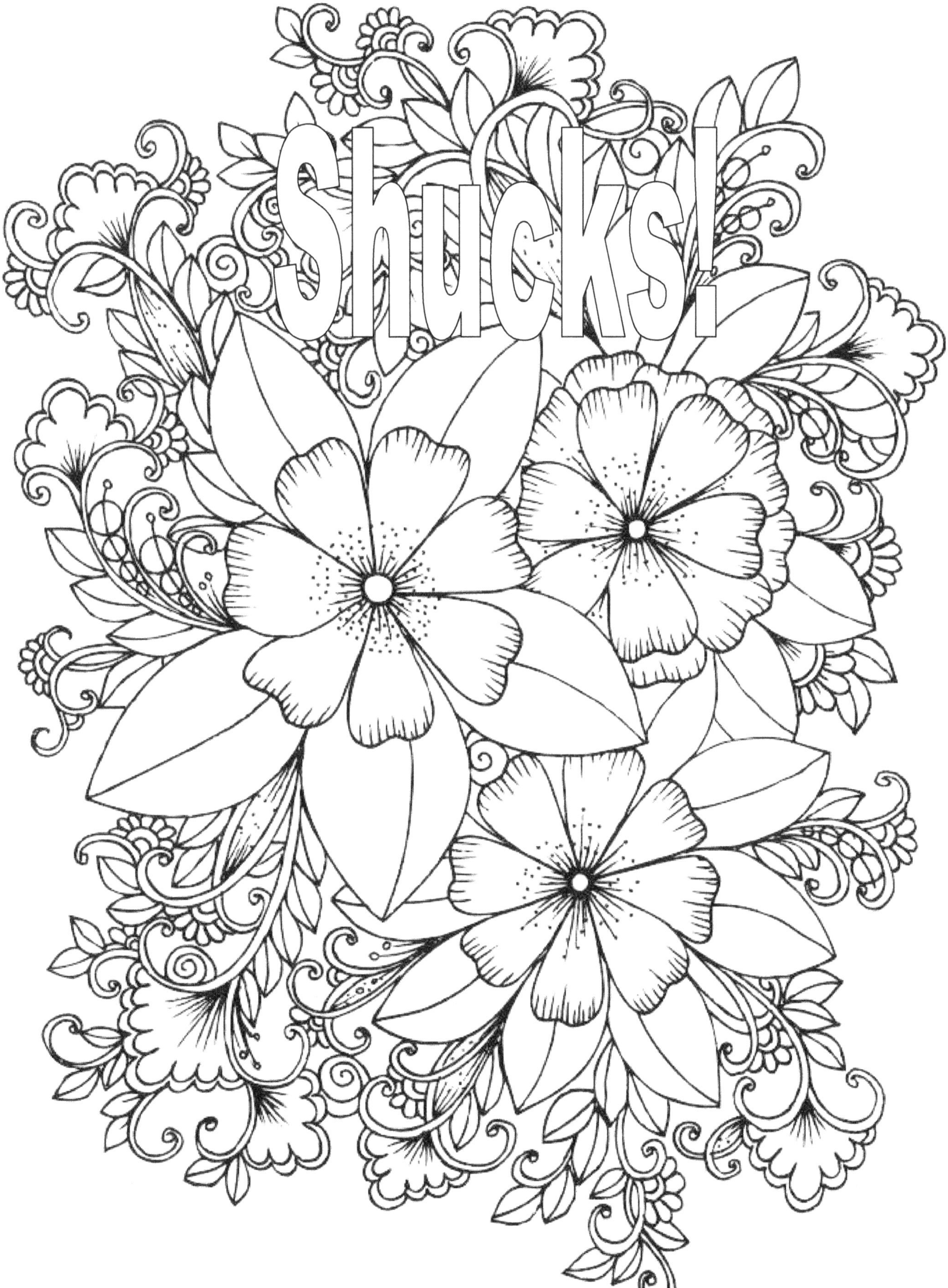
Shucks!

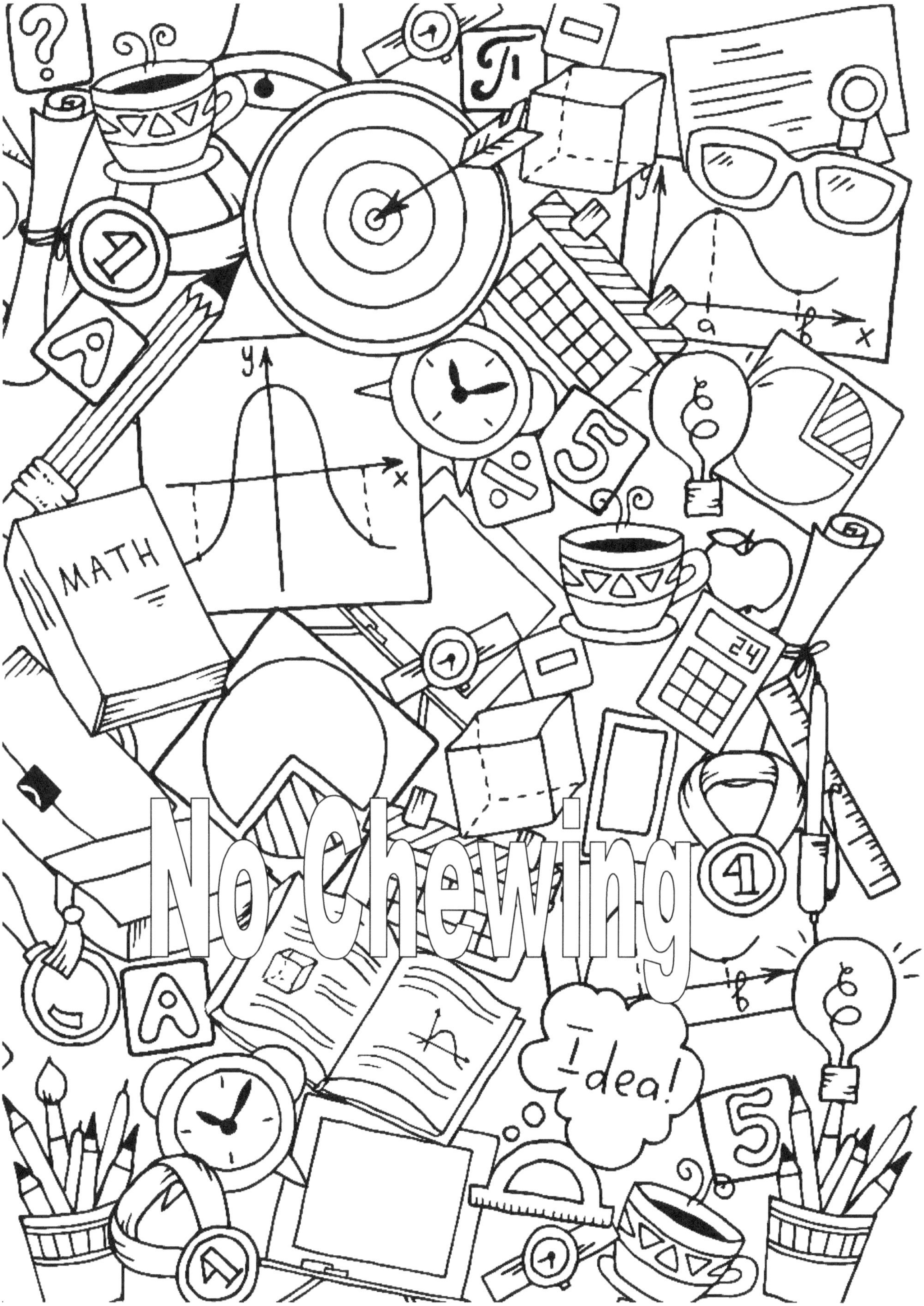
No Chewing
MATH
Idea!

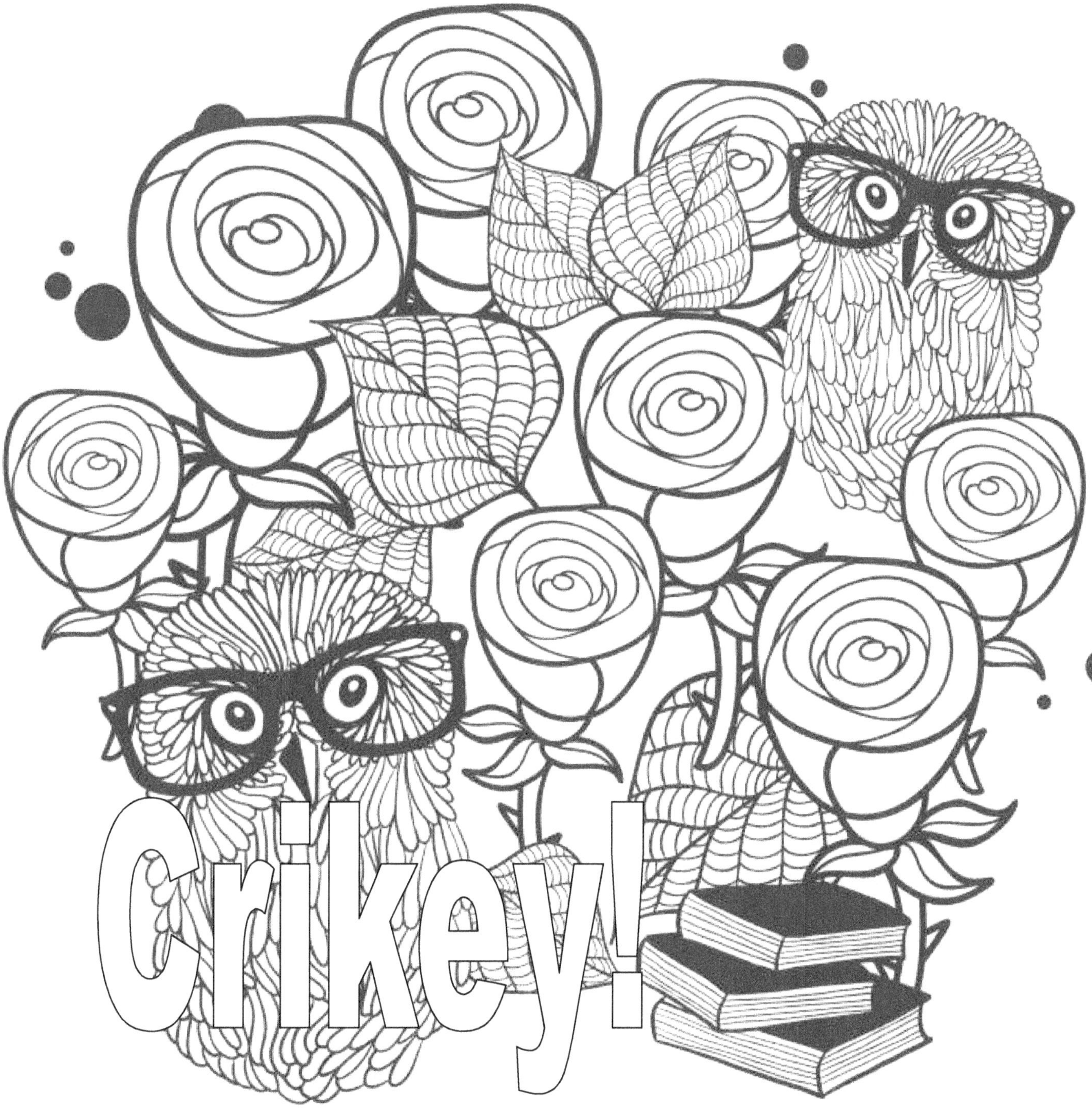
Crikey!

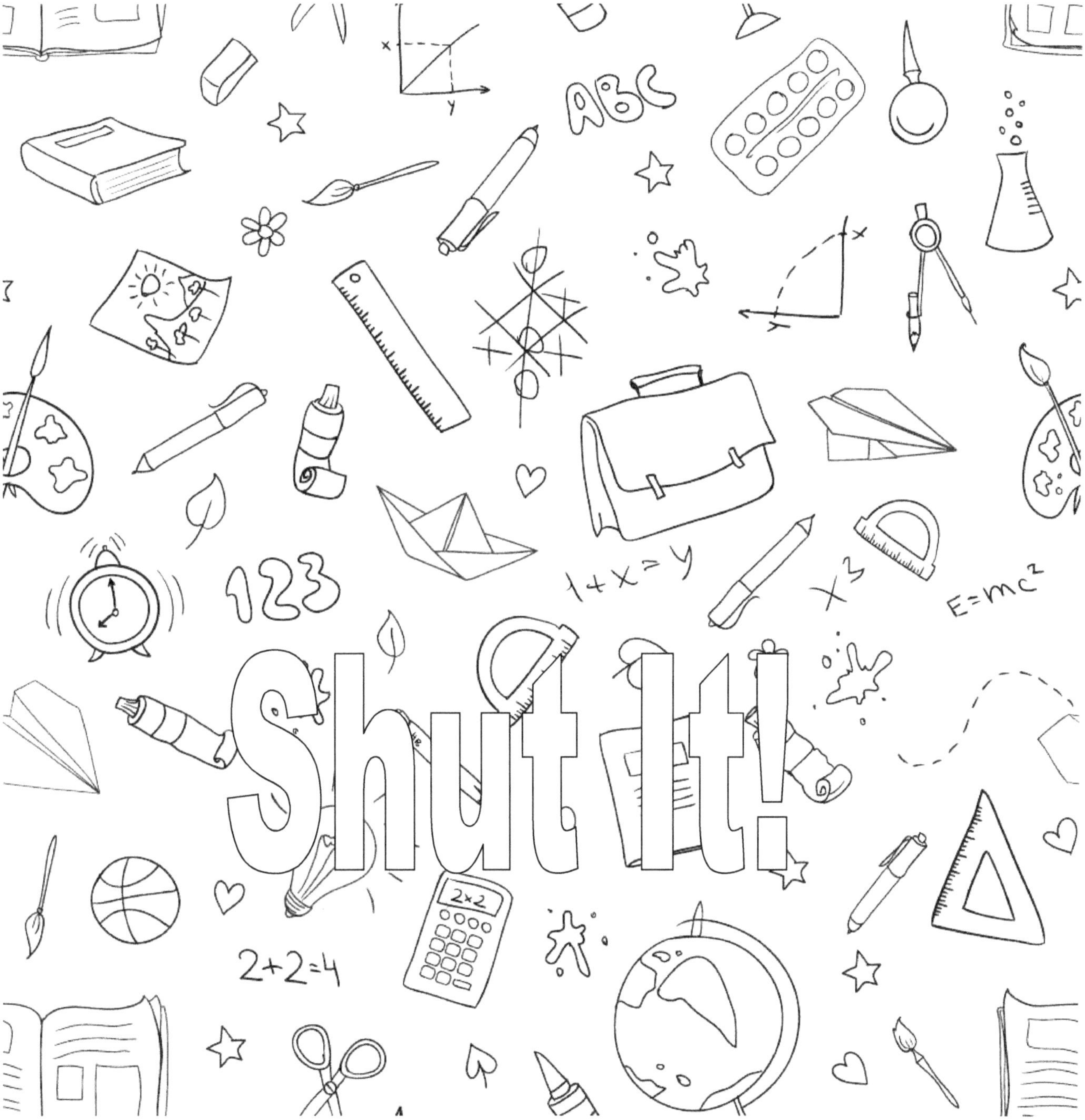
Shut It!
ABC
123
1+x=y
x^3
$E=mc^2$
2+2=4
2×2

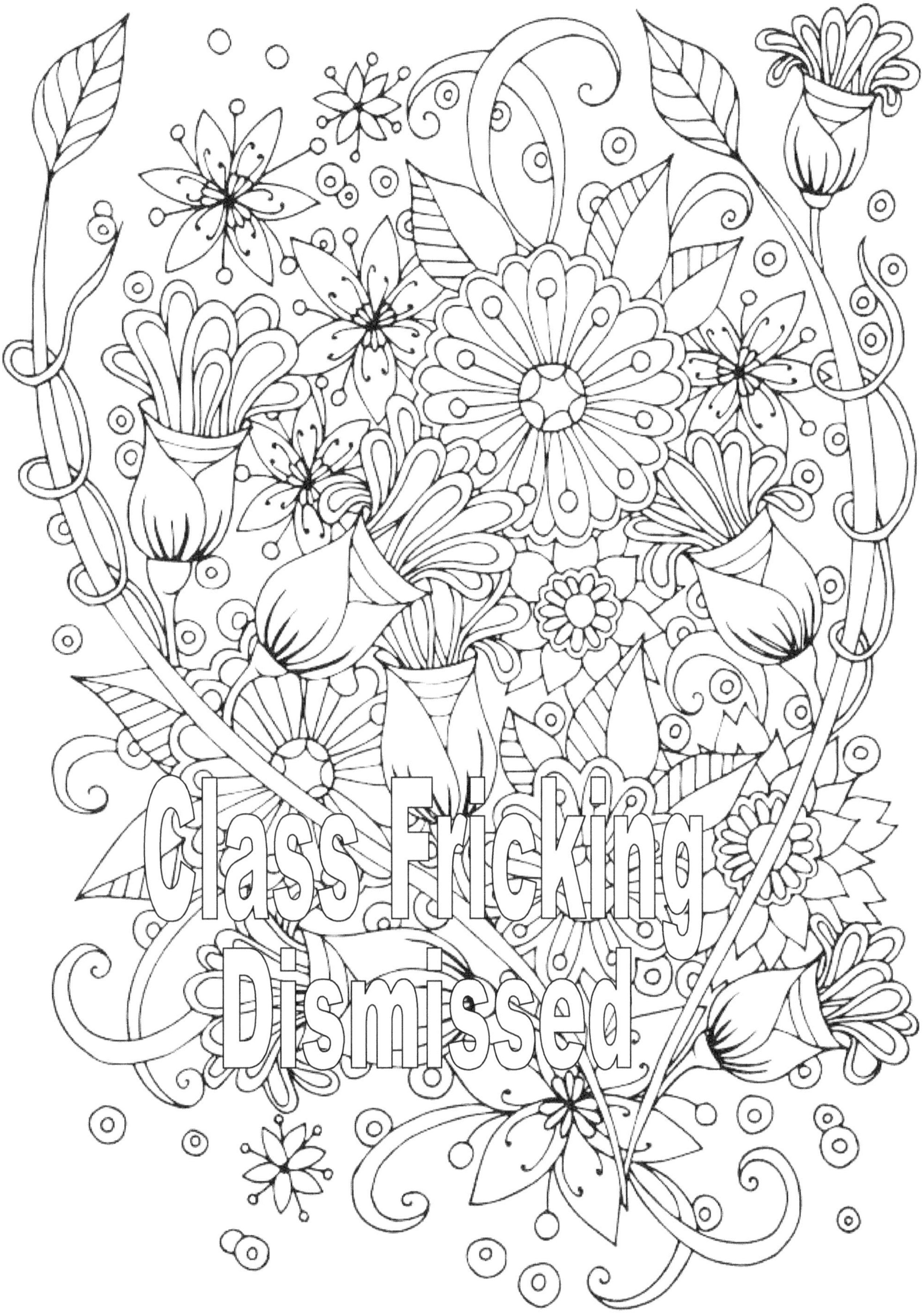
Class Fricking
Dismissed

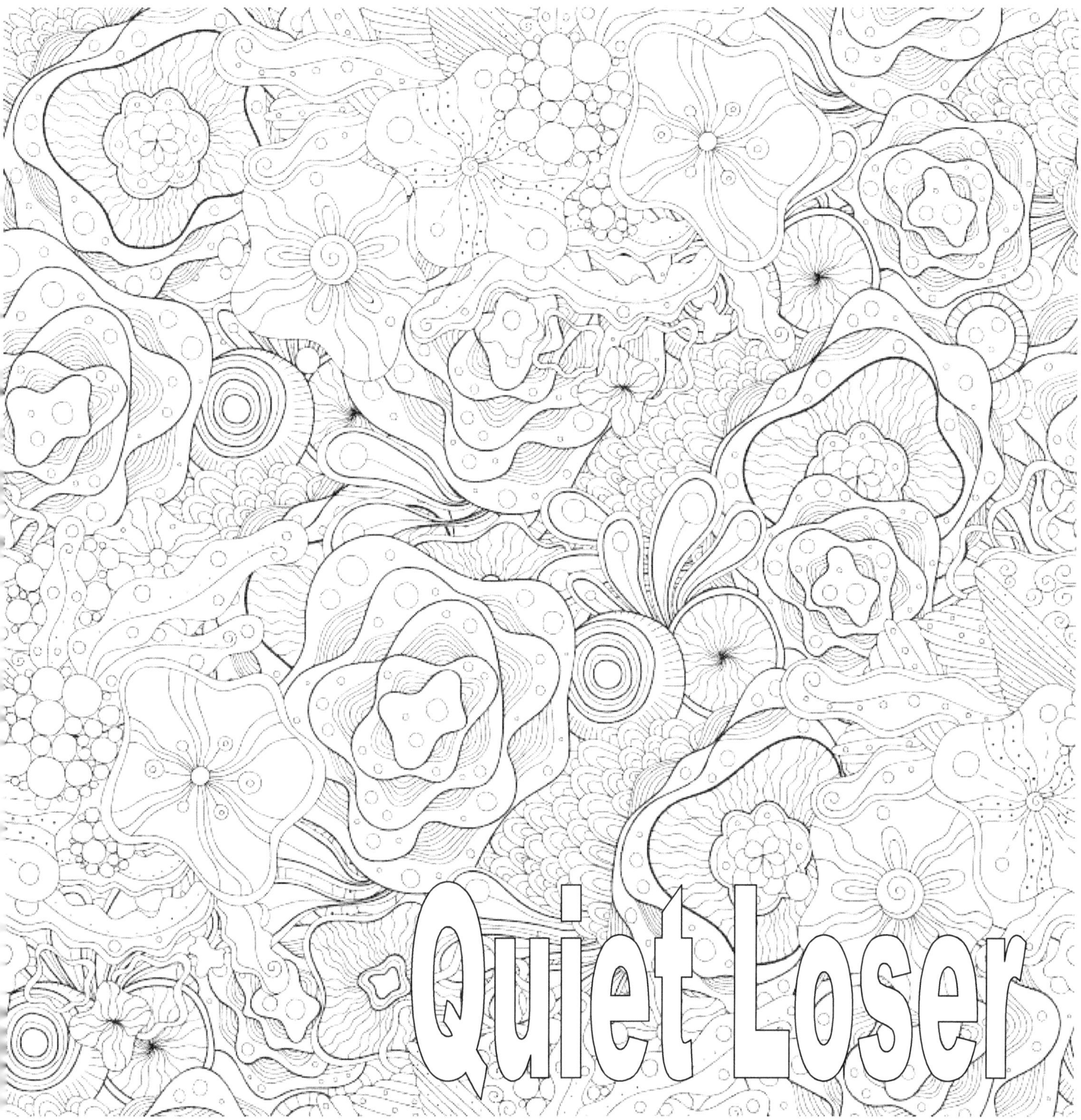
Quiet Loser

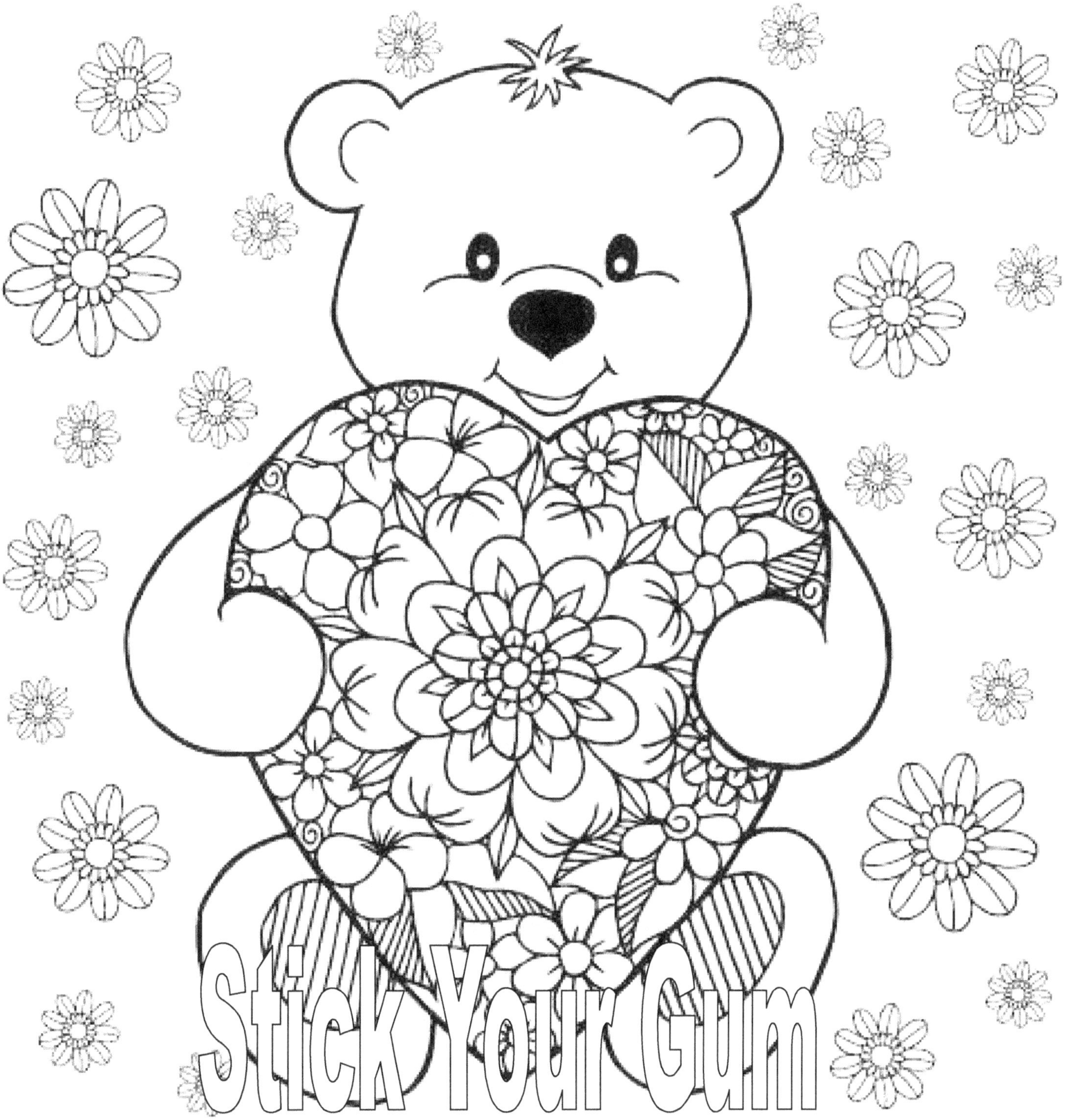
Stick Your Gum

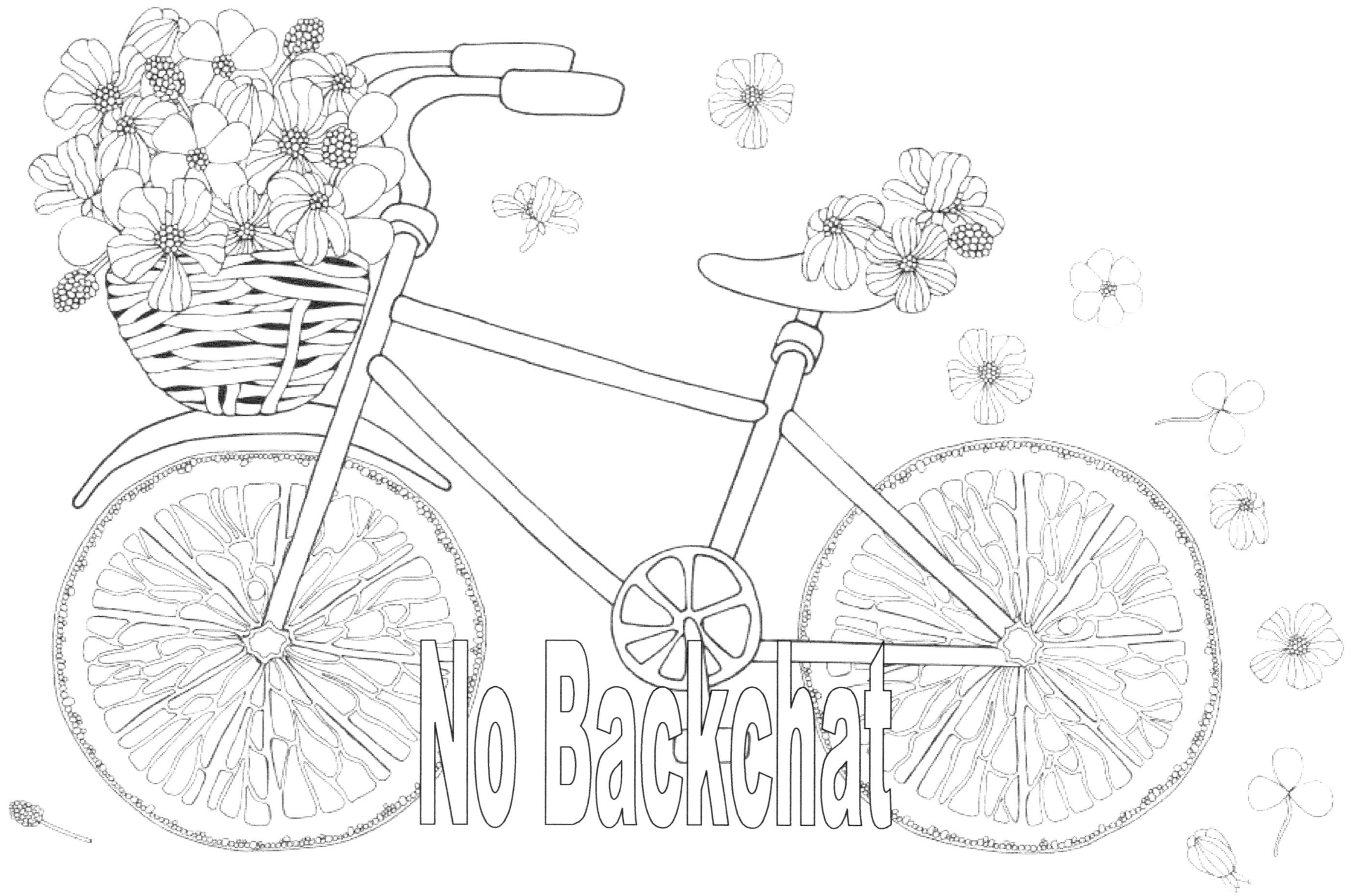
No Backchat

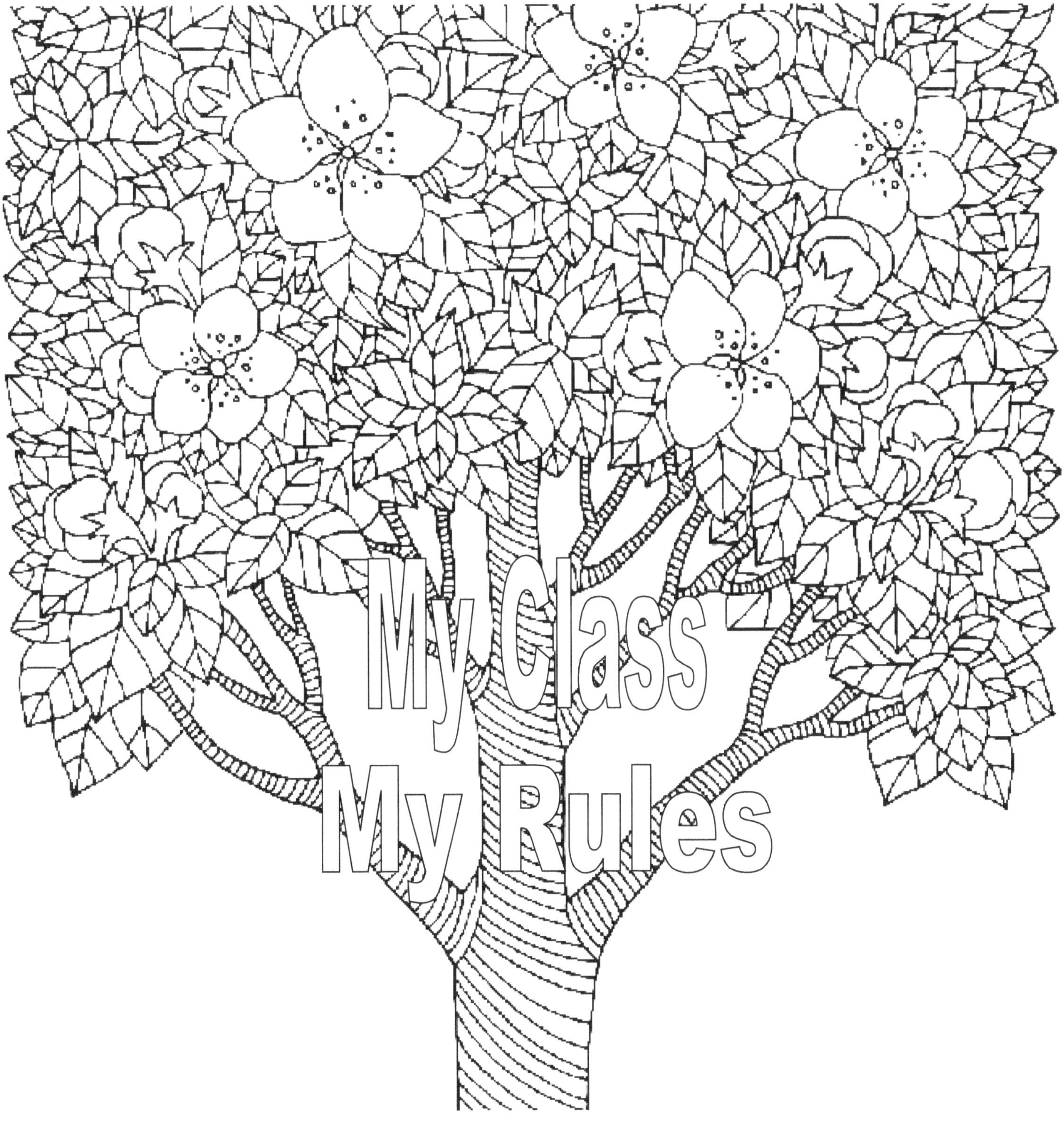
My Class
My Rules

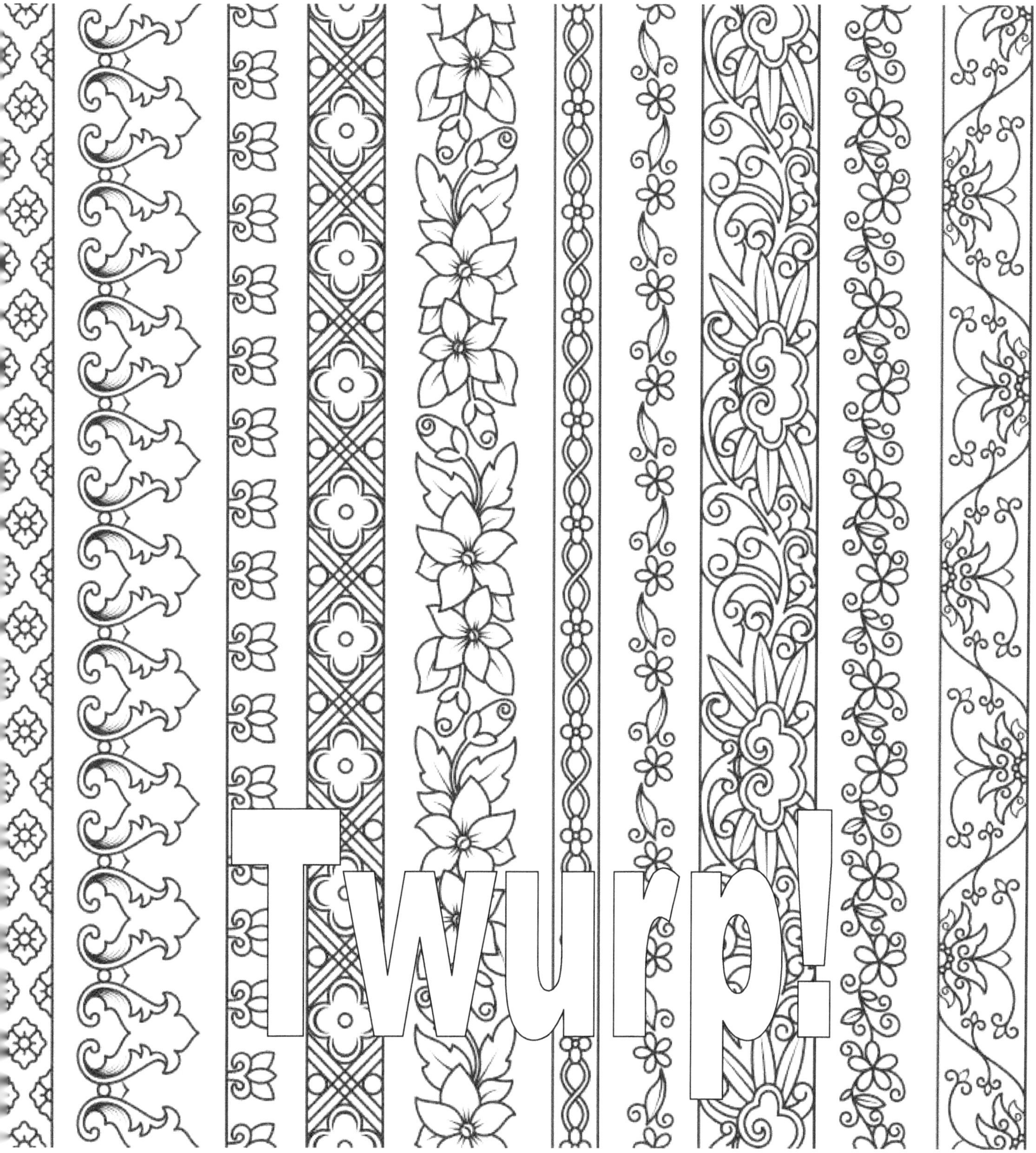
Twurp!

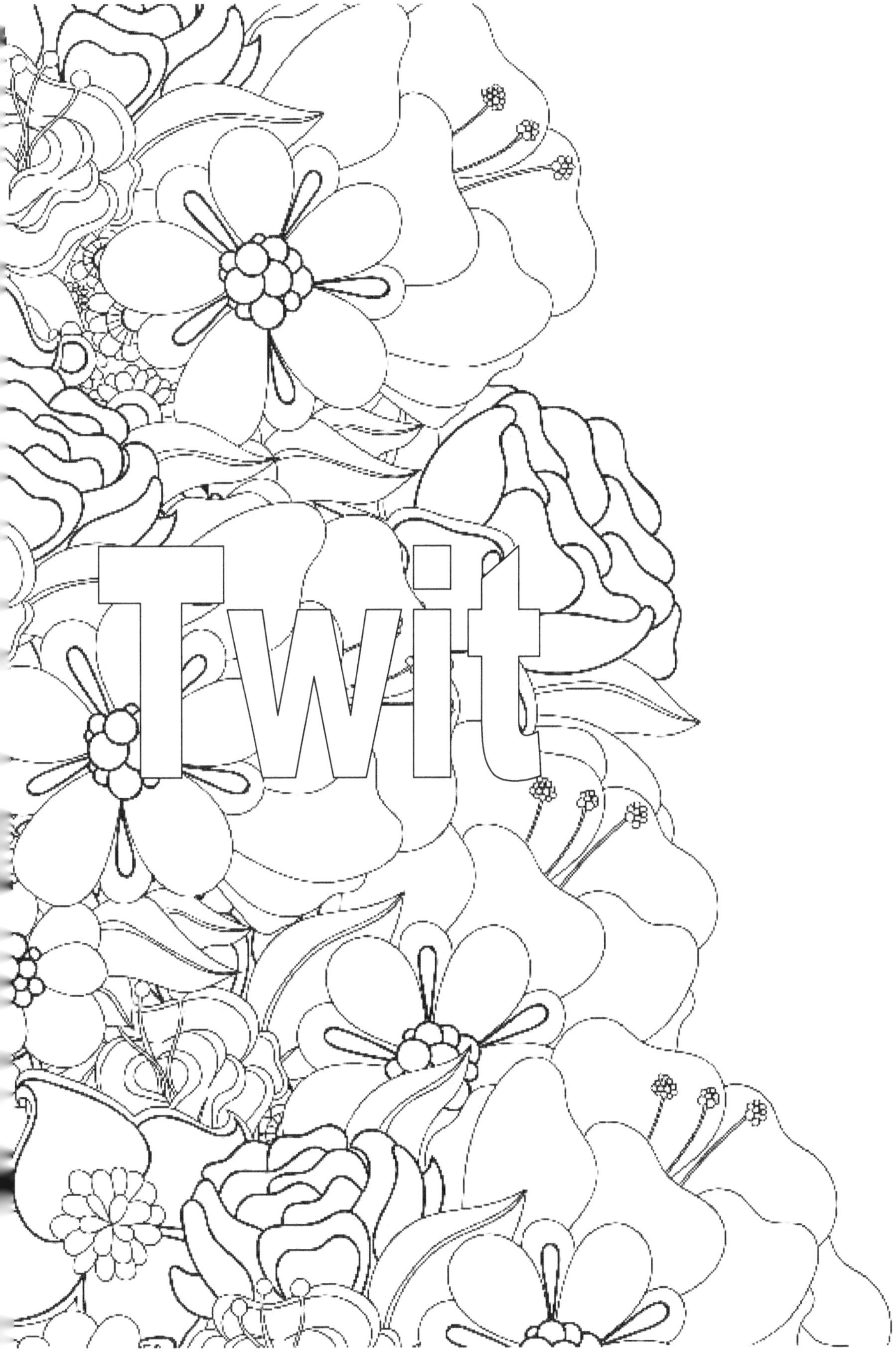
Twit

Surprise Teacher Bonus Calming Sea Turtles Coloring Pages.

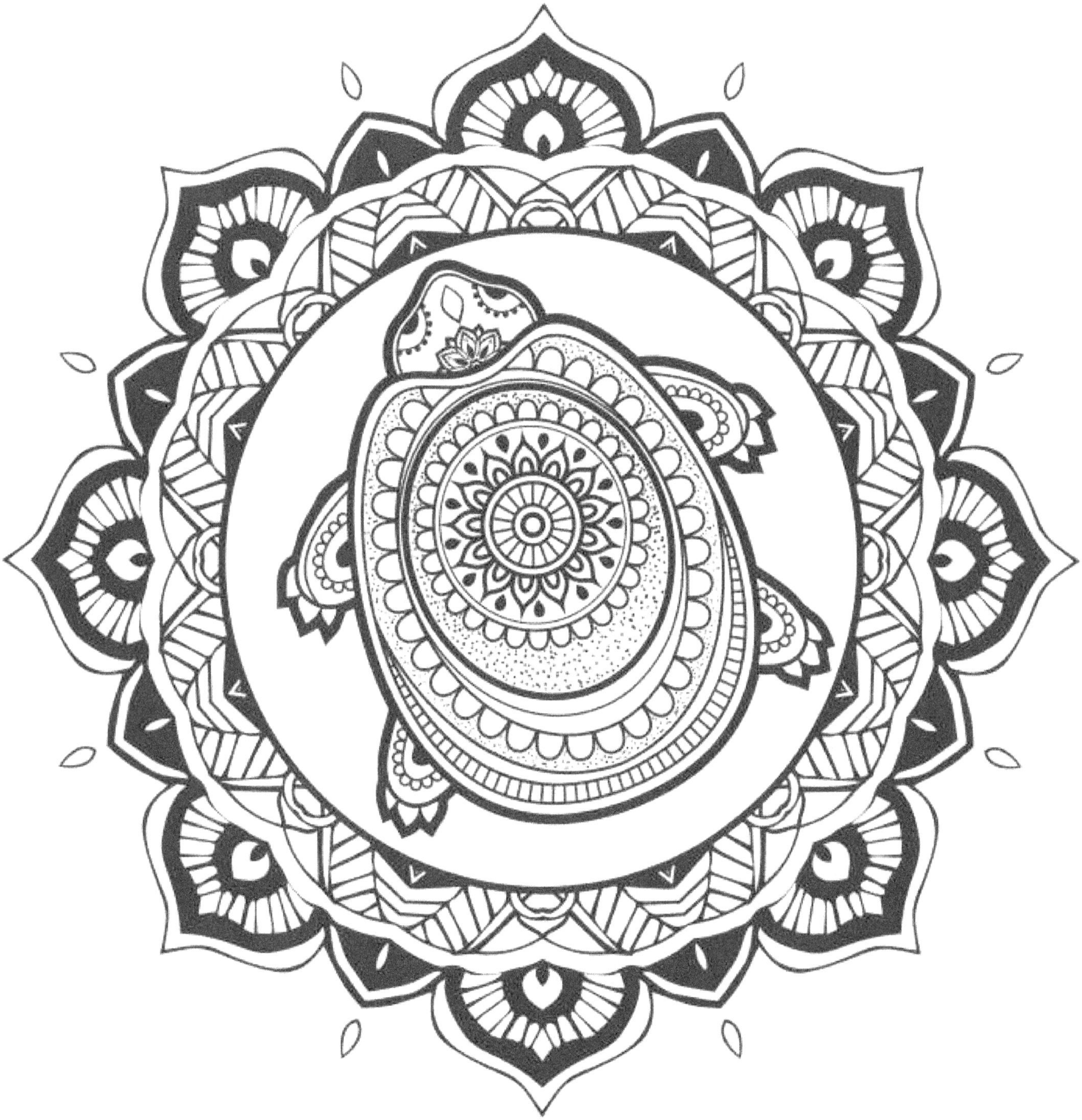

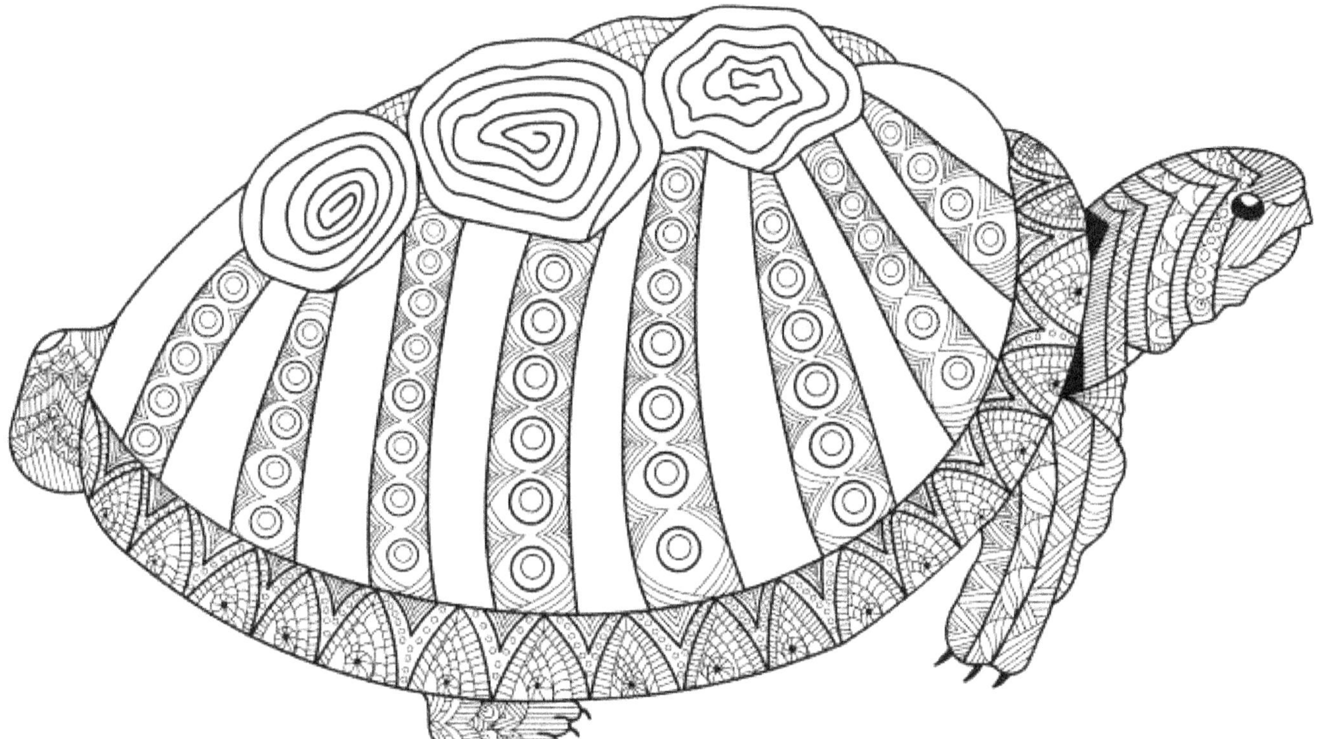

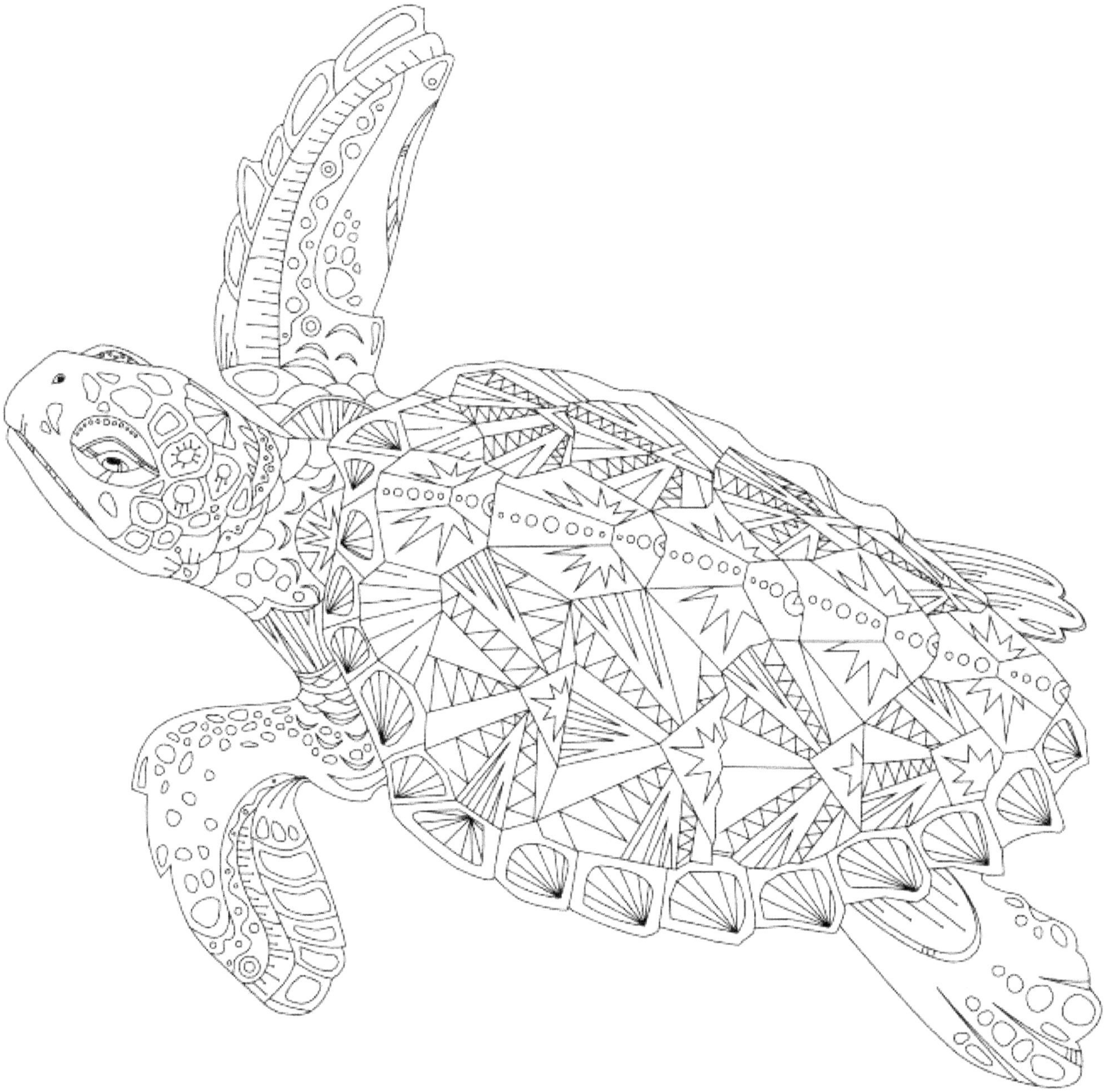

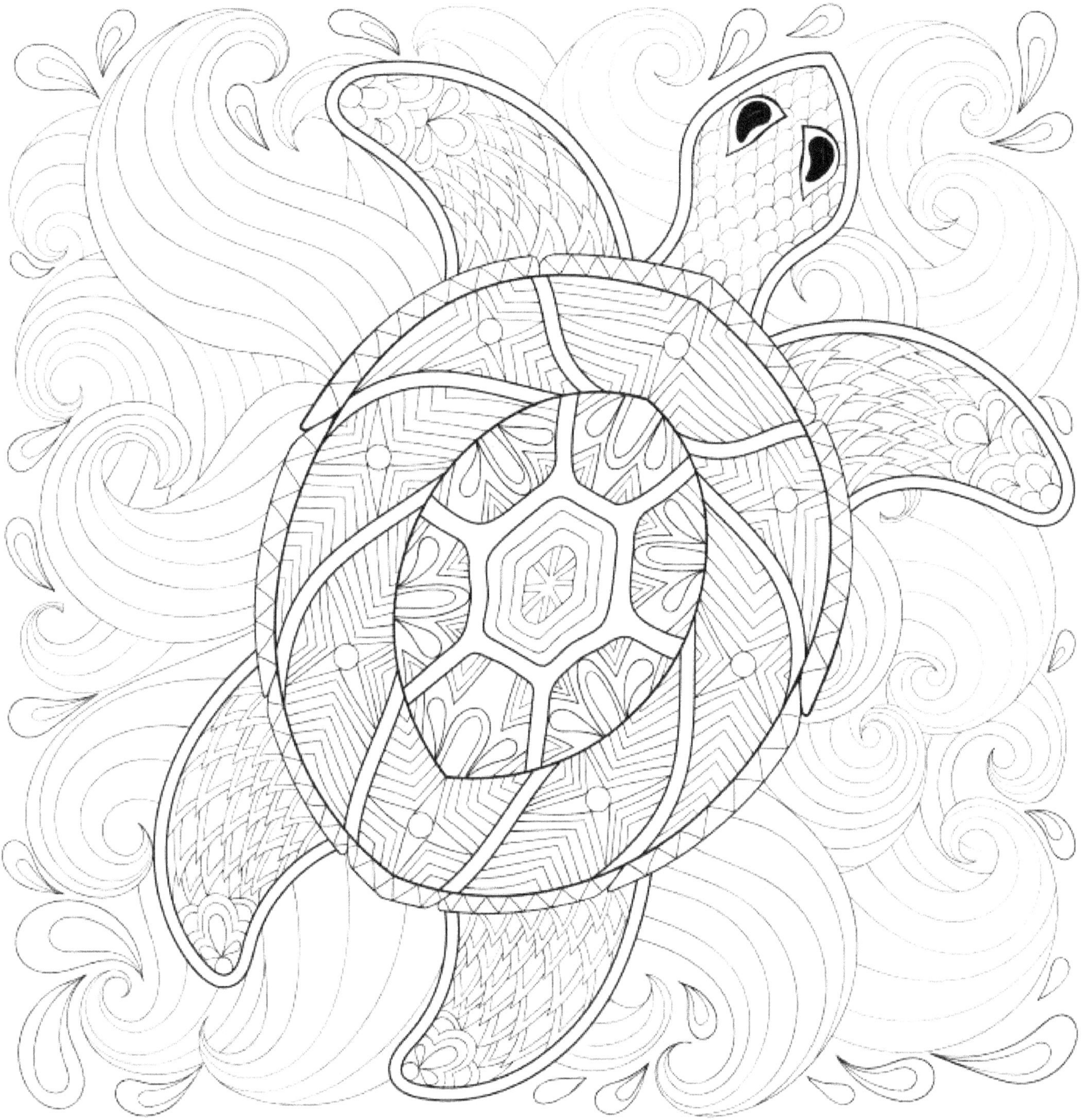

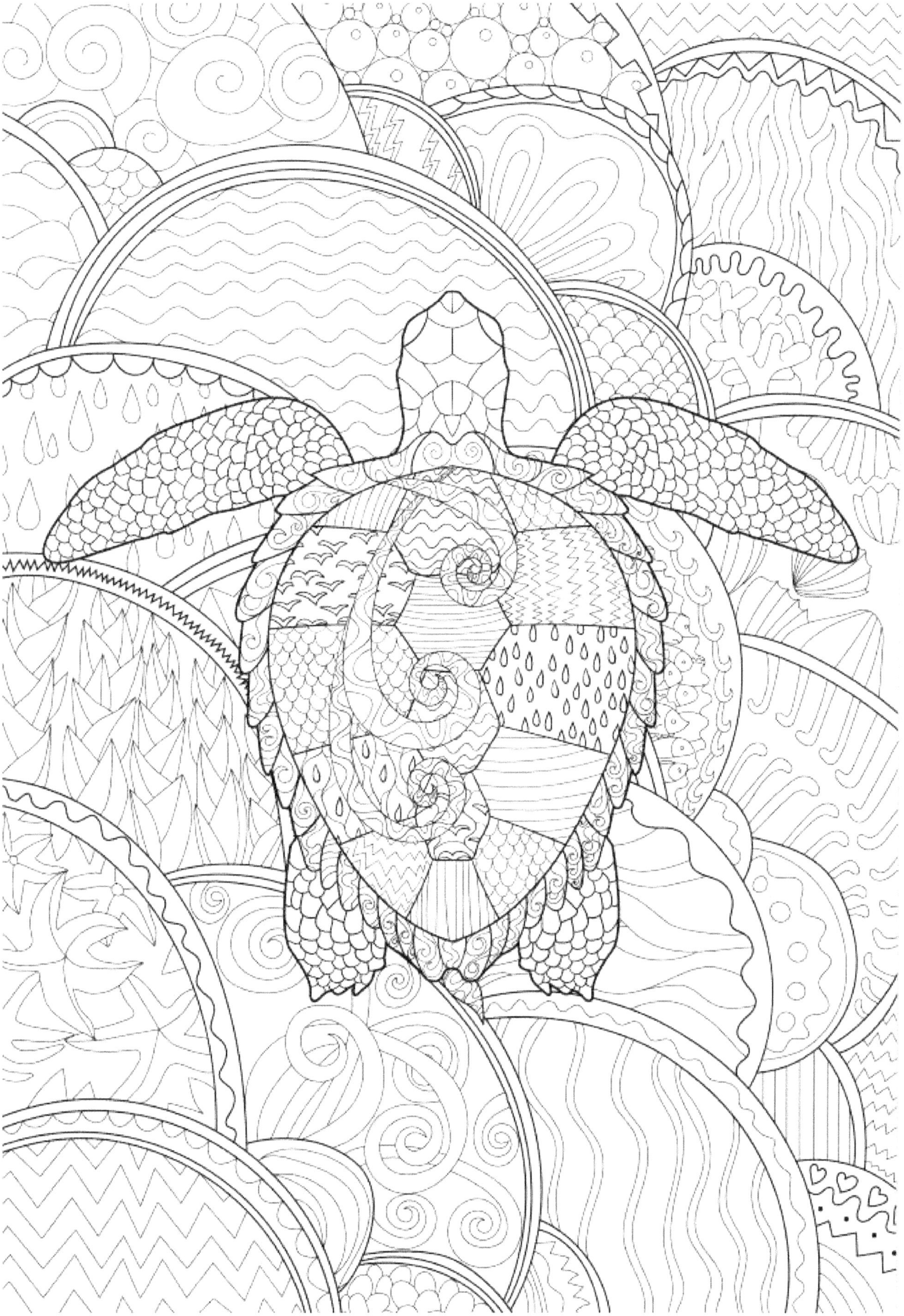

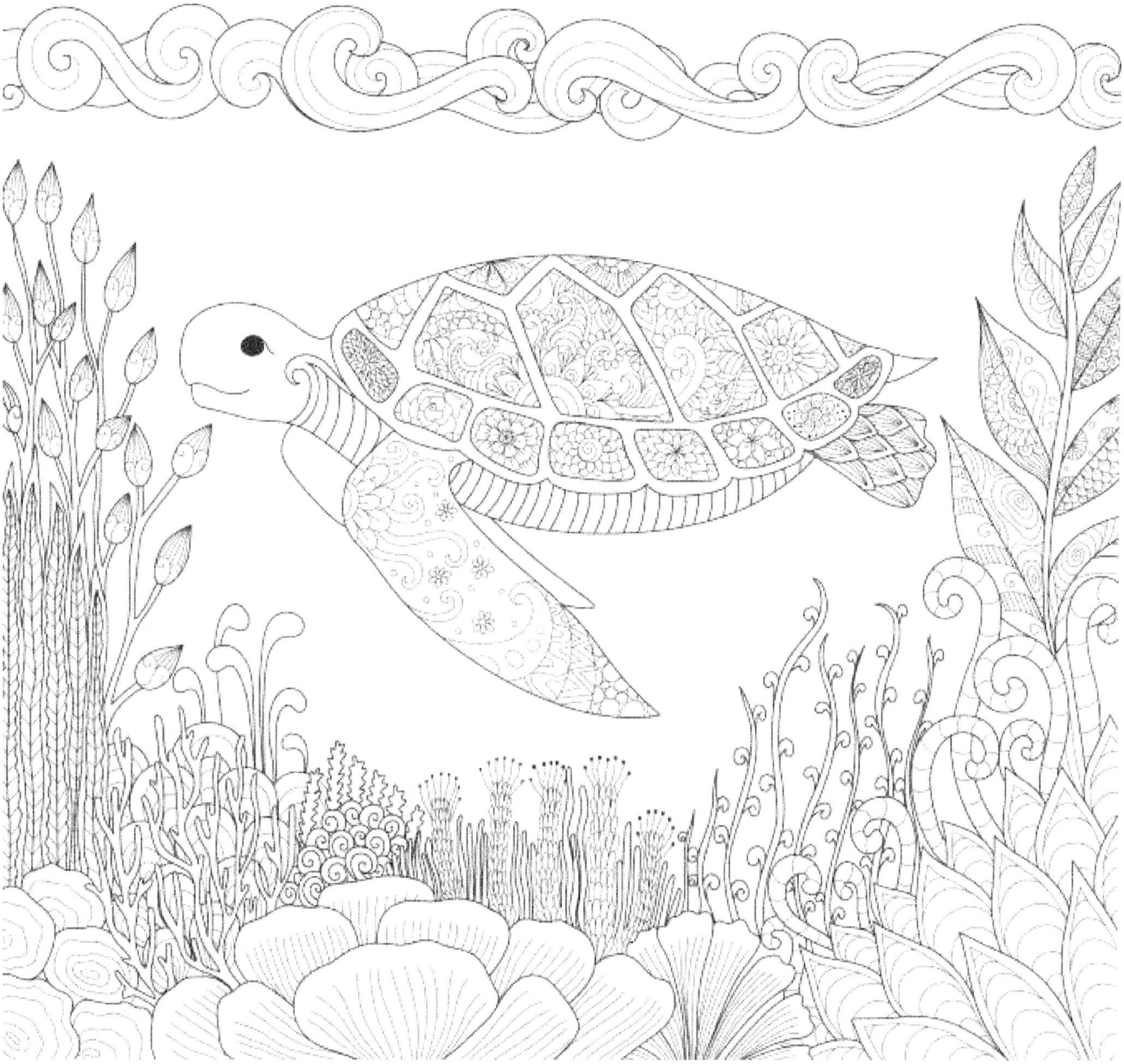

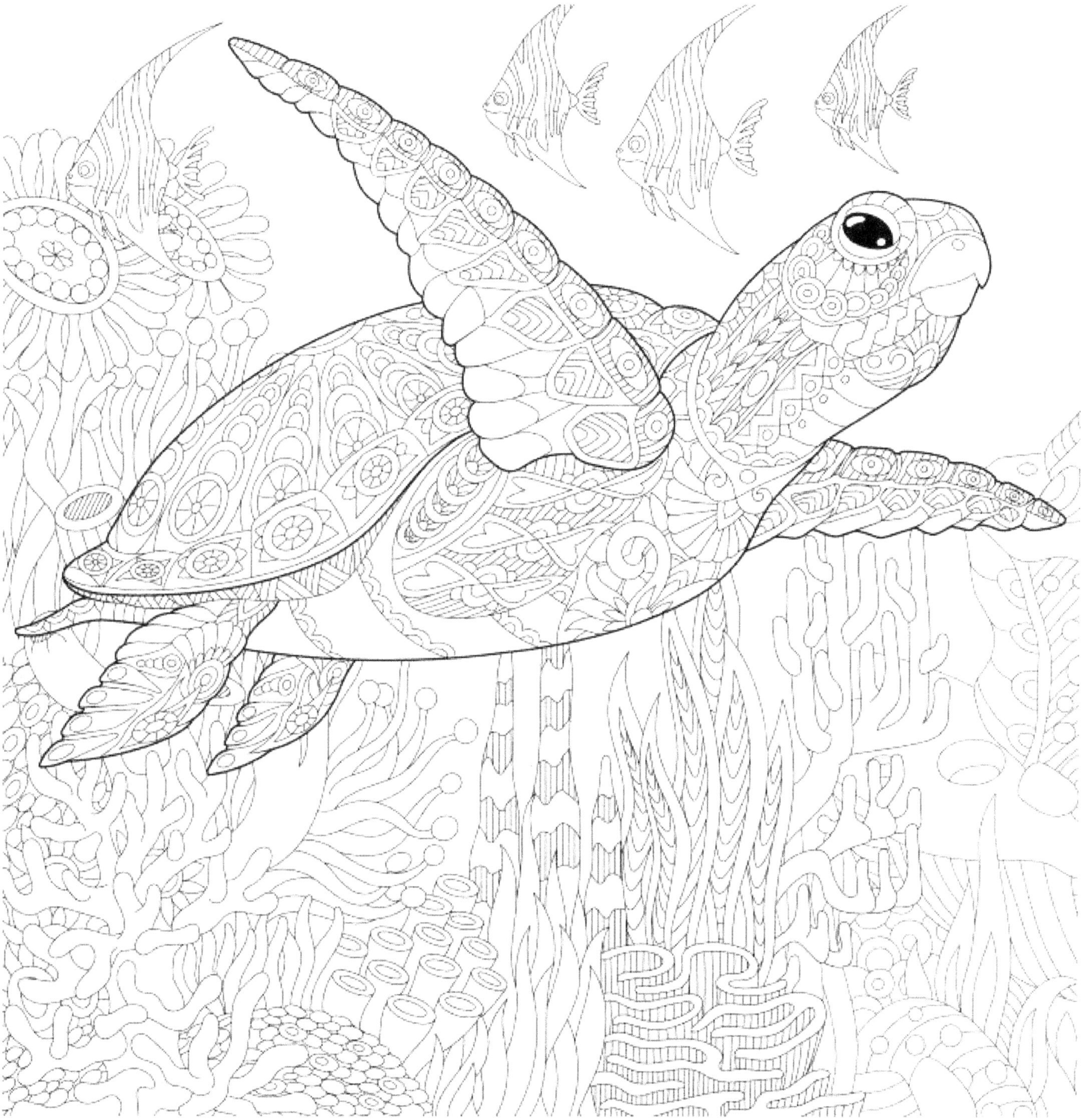

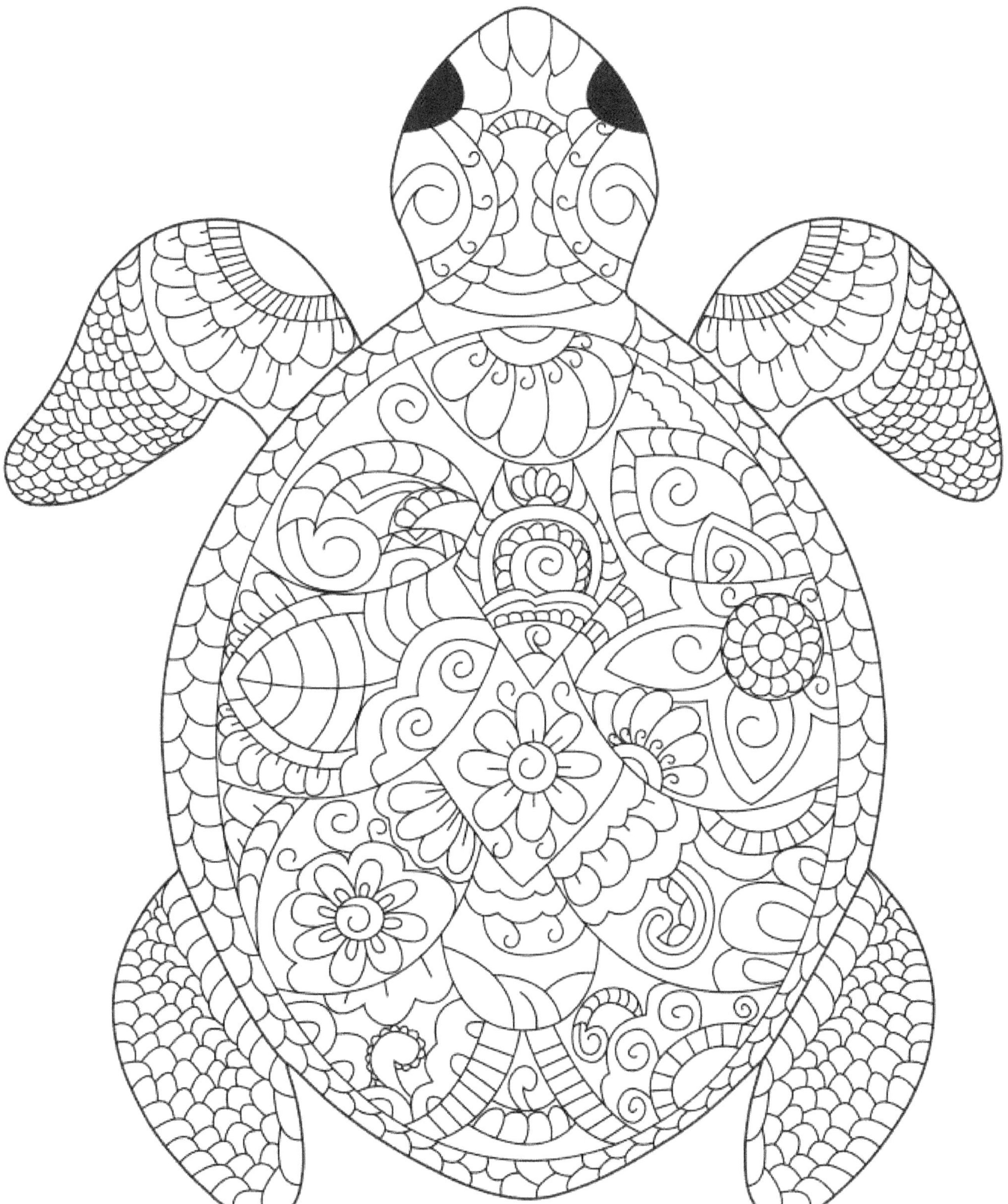

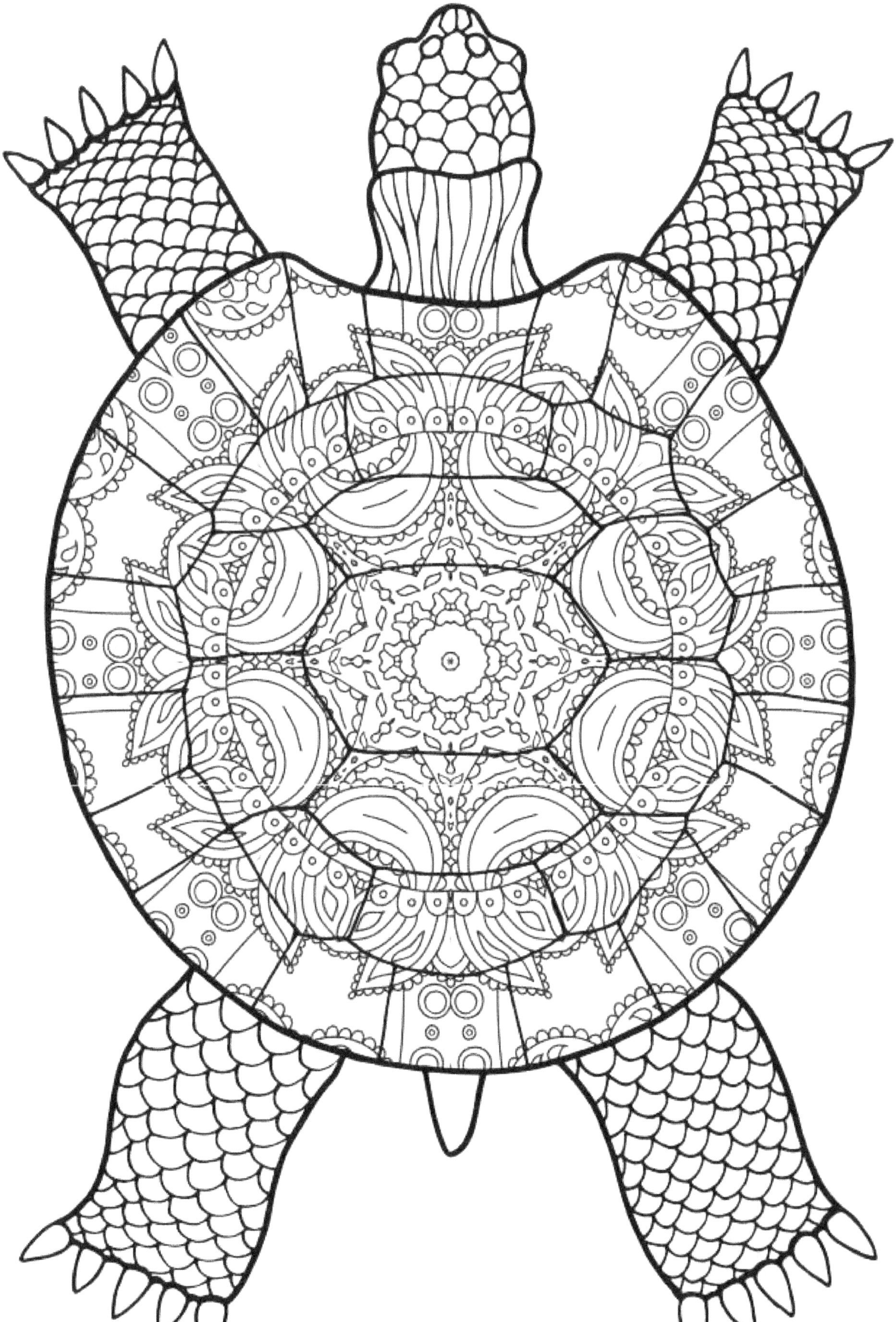

www.ingramcontent.com/pod-product-compliance
Lightning Source LLC
Chambersburg PA
CBHW081303180526
45170CB00007B/2540
* 9 7 8 1 5 4 6 9 8 4 5 3 5 *